In 2018 I have visited Myanmar for a while. Like in many other places, I took interest into the people, what they do, how they look like. In those who come into your sight but that you, tourist eager to see everything, never notice; those people that are the country, the monks (here), the students, the street sellers etc.

Nonetheless taking clear photos of them with a proper camera, even by just having it pending from my neck, would have meant forgetting the spontaneous behavior.
Fortunately nowadays mobiles are so common that having it in your hand gets completely unnoticed. Then you can, with a bit of luck, take some photos.

Here you have it, stolen blinks of reality in Myanmar

Juh Lee Ho & Henry Kwoh

Myanmar, aka Burma, is a fascinating country. Especially at the eyes of a tourist, and not only for the enchanting pagodas and scenarios.

For many it's the symbol of human resilience. Stoically enduring the military occupation of their daily lives, they came out victorious.

Yet it is more than that.

Here if you want to get a glimpse, a bite, of the place, you must look at the streets, at the people filling them and their lives.

They are their traditions, their heritages, their religions, and carry the heavy burden of their pasts while looking at the future ahead.

Myanmar is its own people, both good and bad. Poor and rich, soldiers and gardeners, state workers and monks, Buddhists and not.

These are pics of them. Anonymous passers-by in the street; people that stay in your life just for the blink of an eyes, unnoticed.

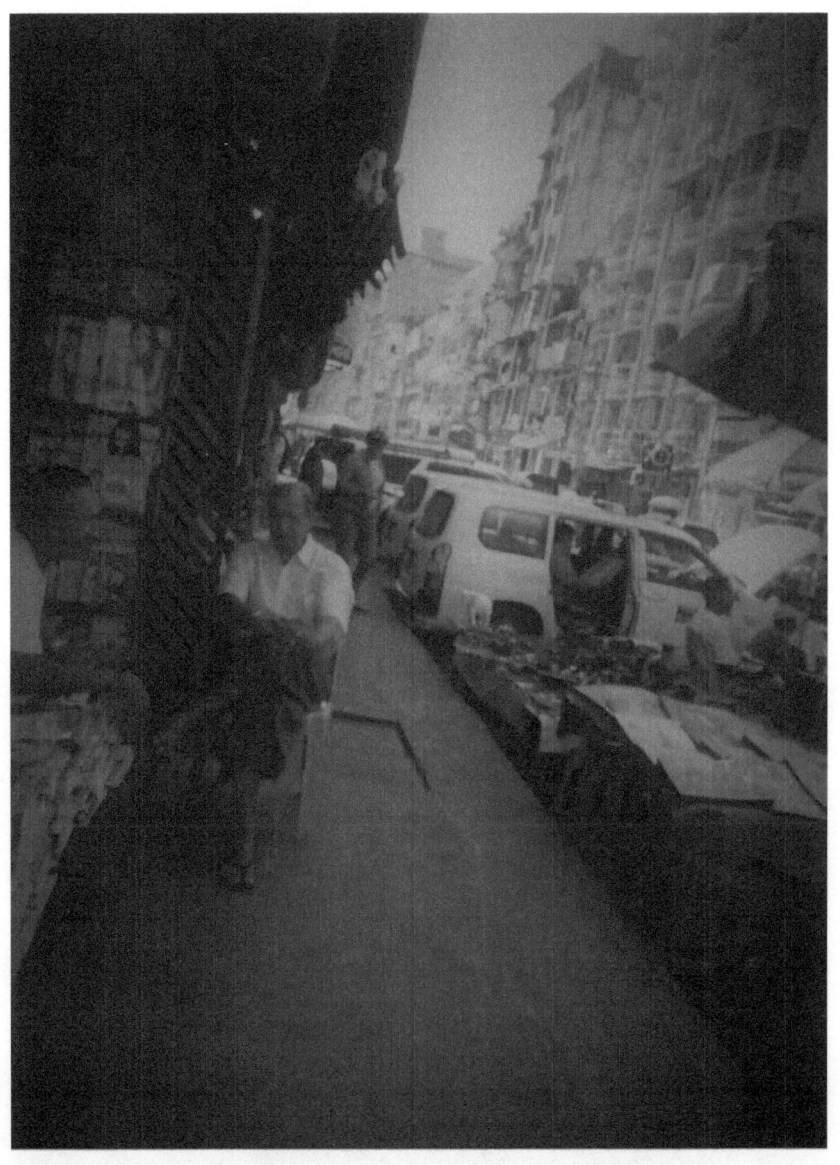

This photo has been taken in the city centre of Yangon (2018)

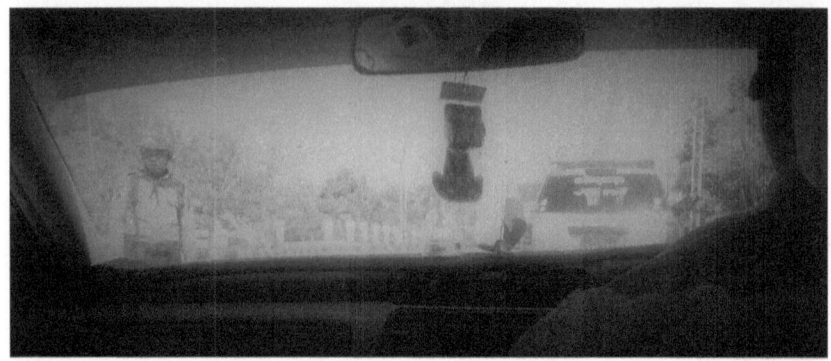

Myanmar meant and sometimes still means soldiers, soldiers to a degree that may resembles paranoia. Nay Pyi Taw is the new official capital and is among such places. It is a city planned by the army and is still heavily controlled.

But somehow you feel that the men with rifles are now out of places there too.

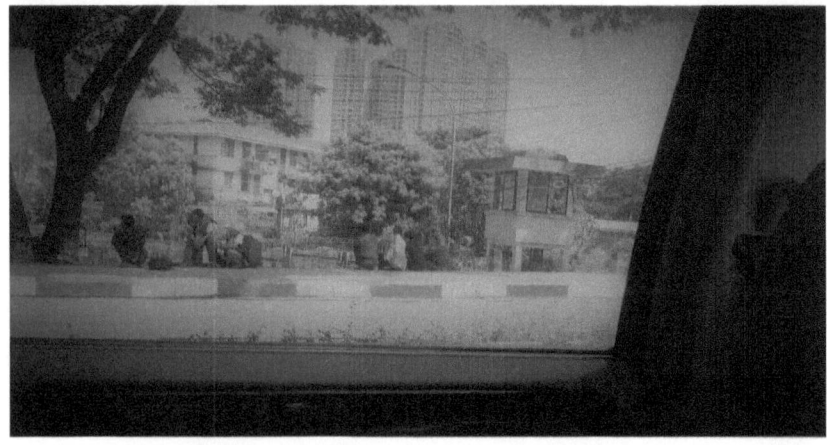

But in other places the army is in total and unconditional retreat. The abandoned watch towers are now only a reminder of the recent past. And of the victory that the human resilience can achieve.

Social Life

Social life, in Myanmar like in any other place on this planet means laughing with your friends; eating when you can with your friends and relatives in places that you know sooner or later will be no more. Regardless of your religion or of your gender.

The following 3 photos has been taken in Nay Pyi Taw (the first) and in Yangon (second the third).

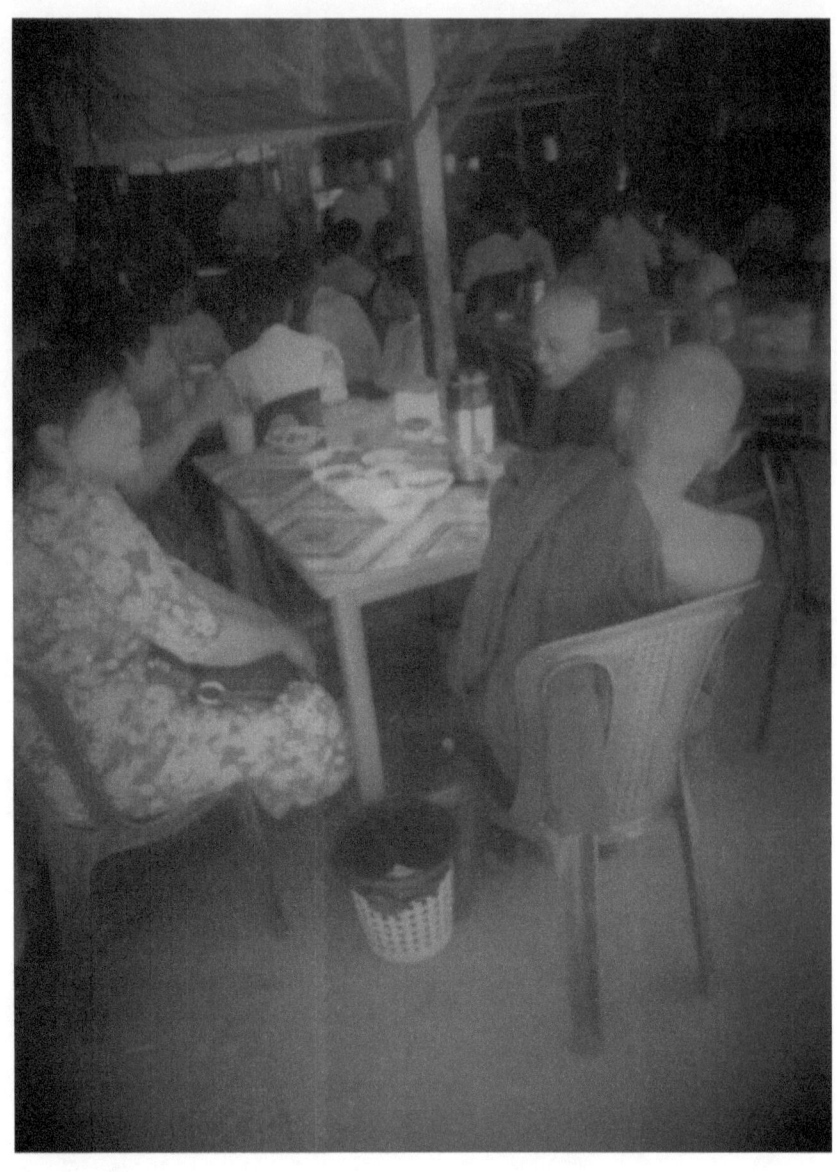

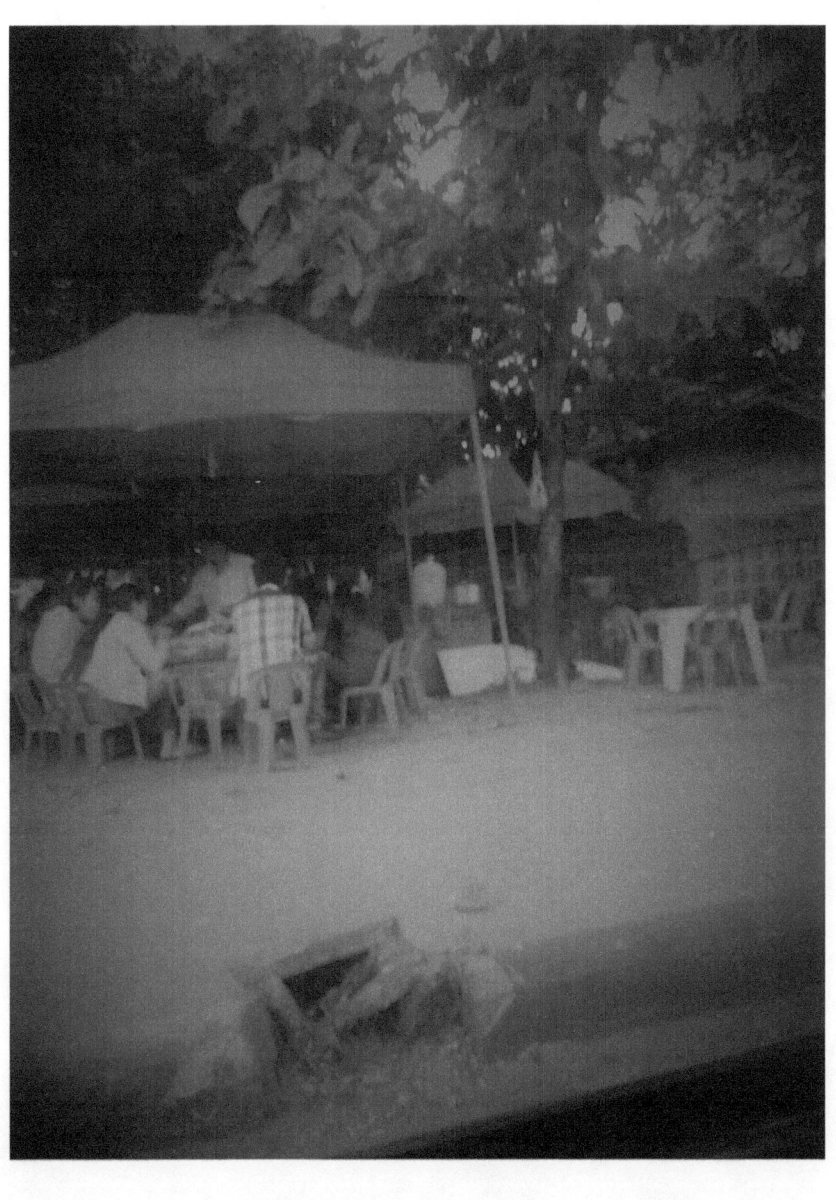

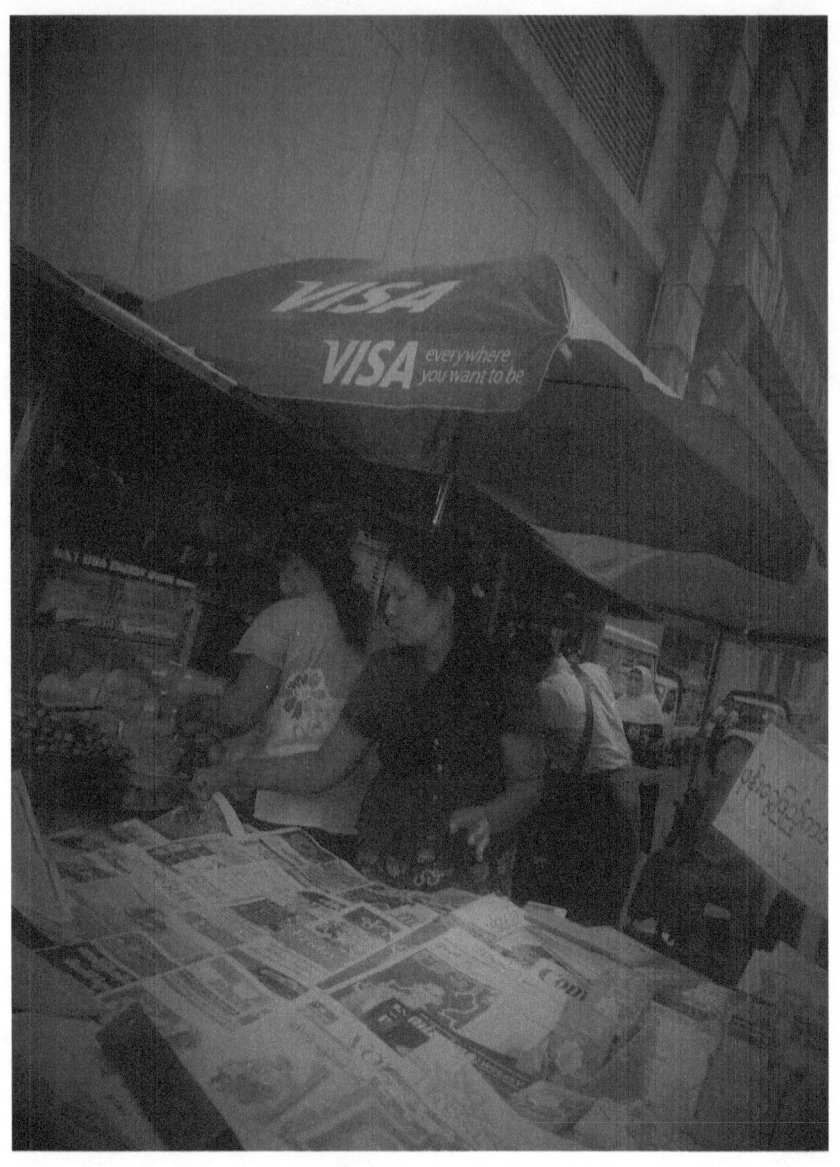

Work Life

In a developing country, especially one that has been frozen for fairly too long, working may mean many different things. Only walking around and noticing you can spot the many different things people do. From working barefooted in a station between two cities, or head down on your humble job with incredible devotion to your duty while nearby new young executive carry on high end jobs (Nay Pyi Taw). It also means coming back from abroad at Rangoon Airport.

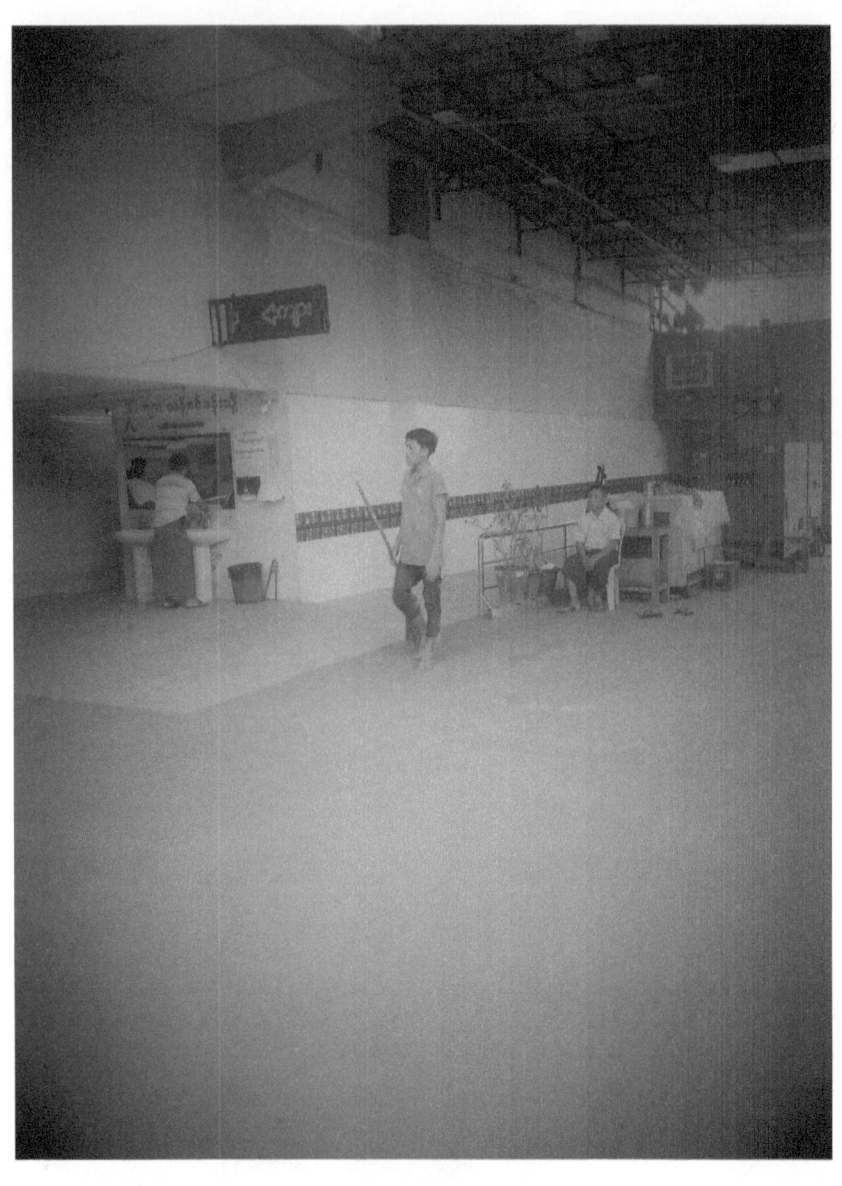

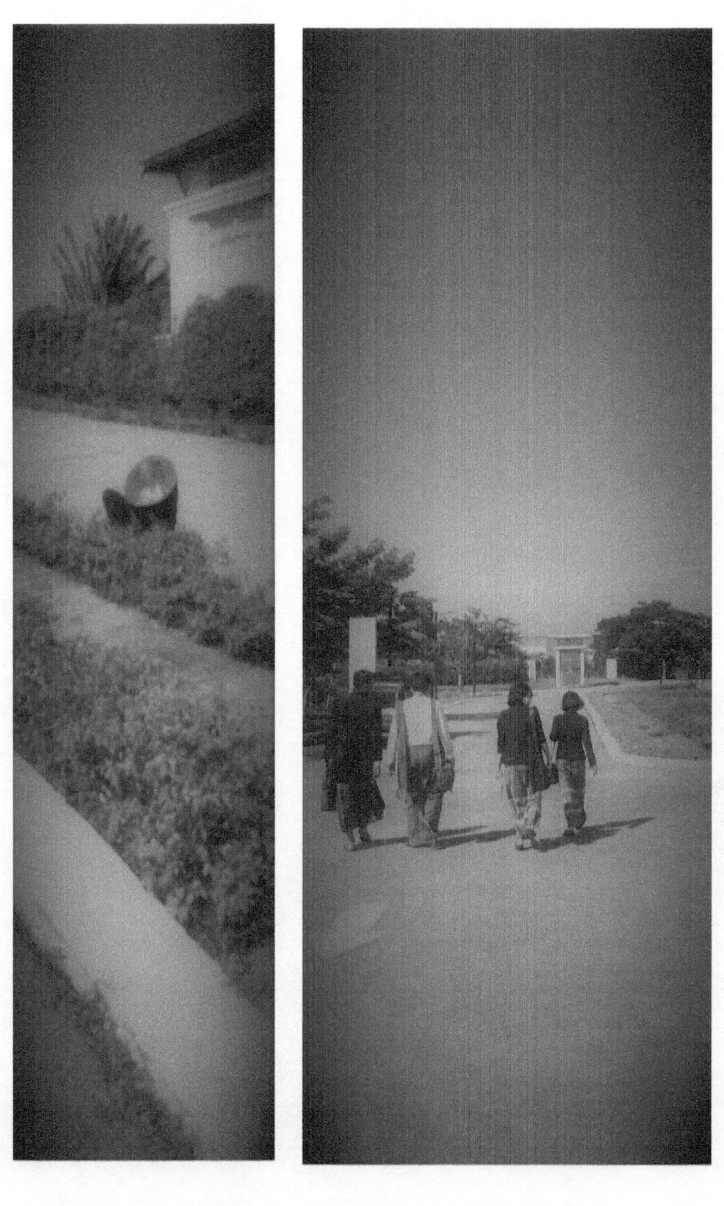

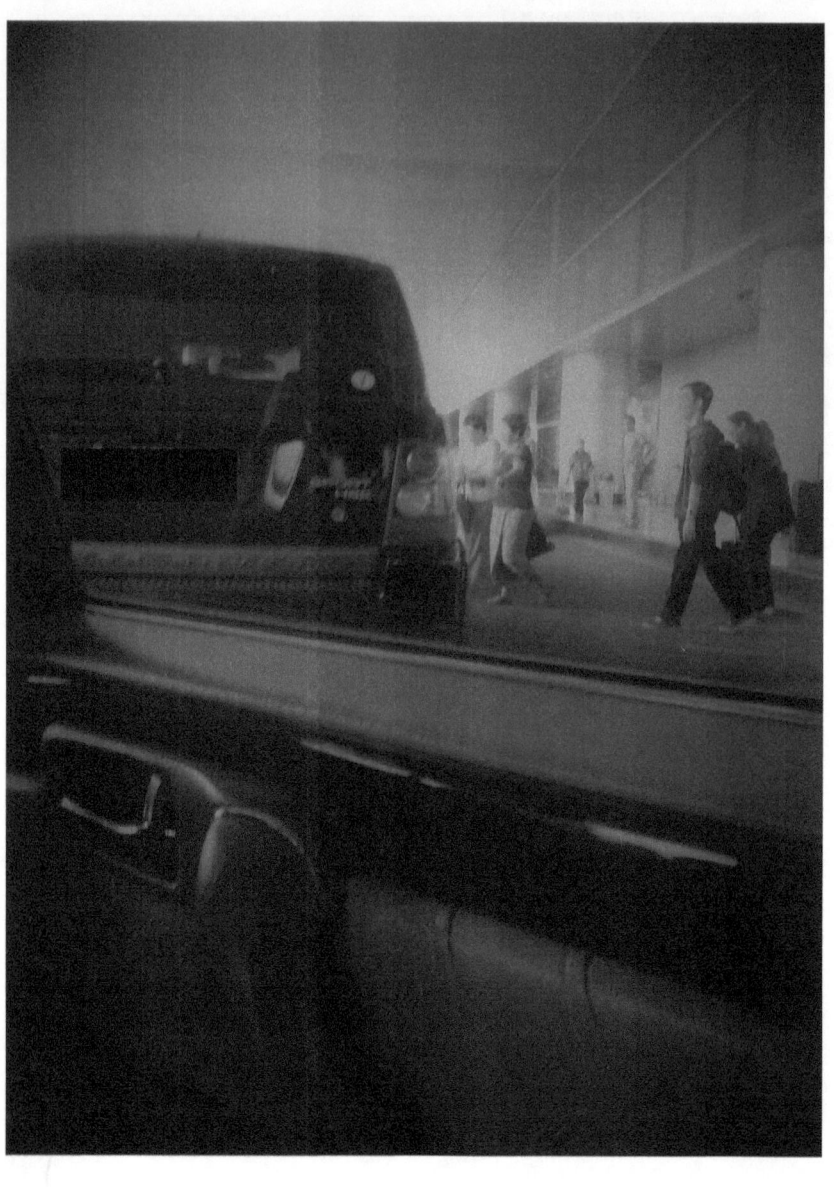

Market Life

No other places are more representative of a country then its markets, night markets like supermarkets, with their incredible life around. People there really live the place and yet, you barely notice anyone. It means going around with your school friend in a night market while a seller plays with his mobile phone while waiting for customers. It means trying to hold on your traditional longyi dress in the escalator. Tradition and modernity may have some issue here to merge smoothly, while in supermarket employees sell, customers buys and ask for help. All photos are from Nay Pyi Taw.

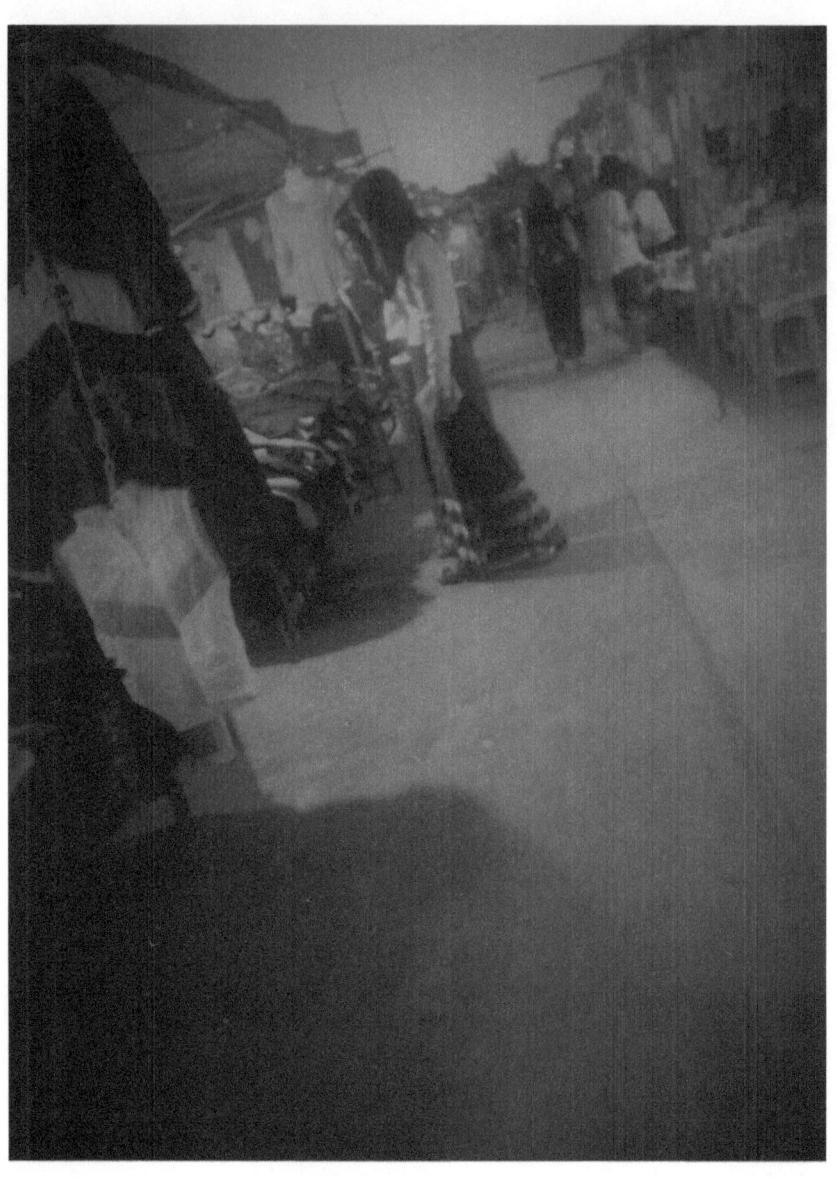

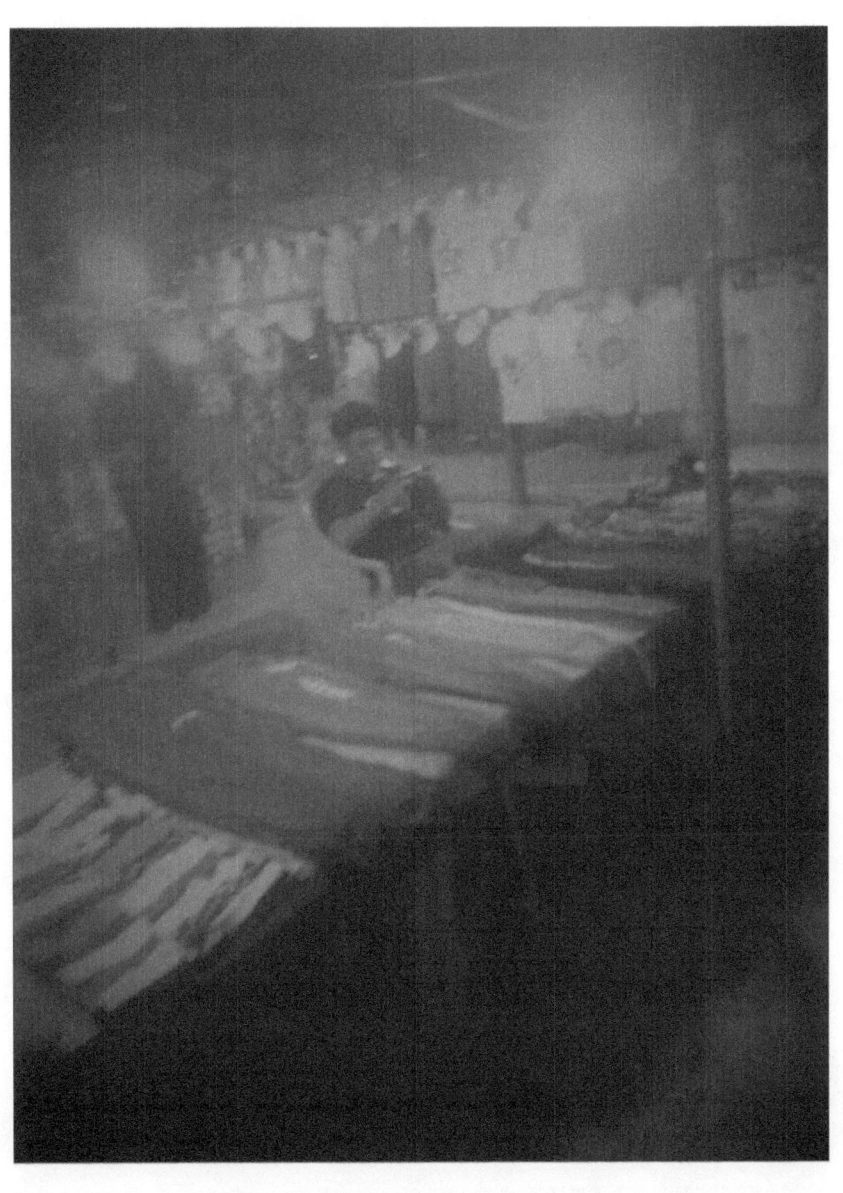

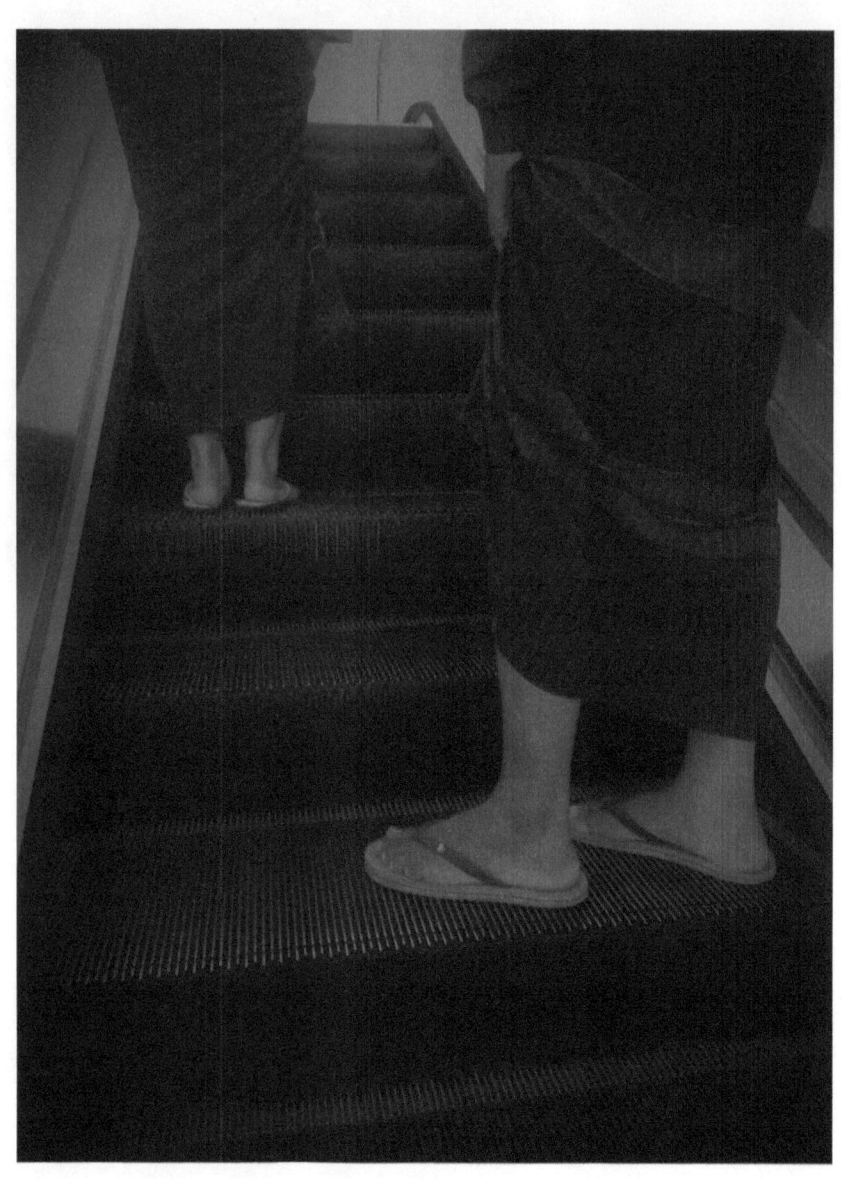

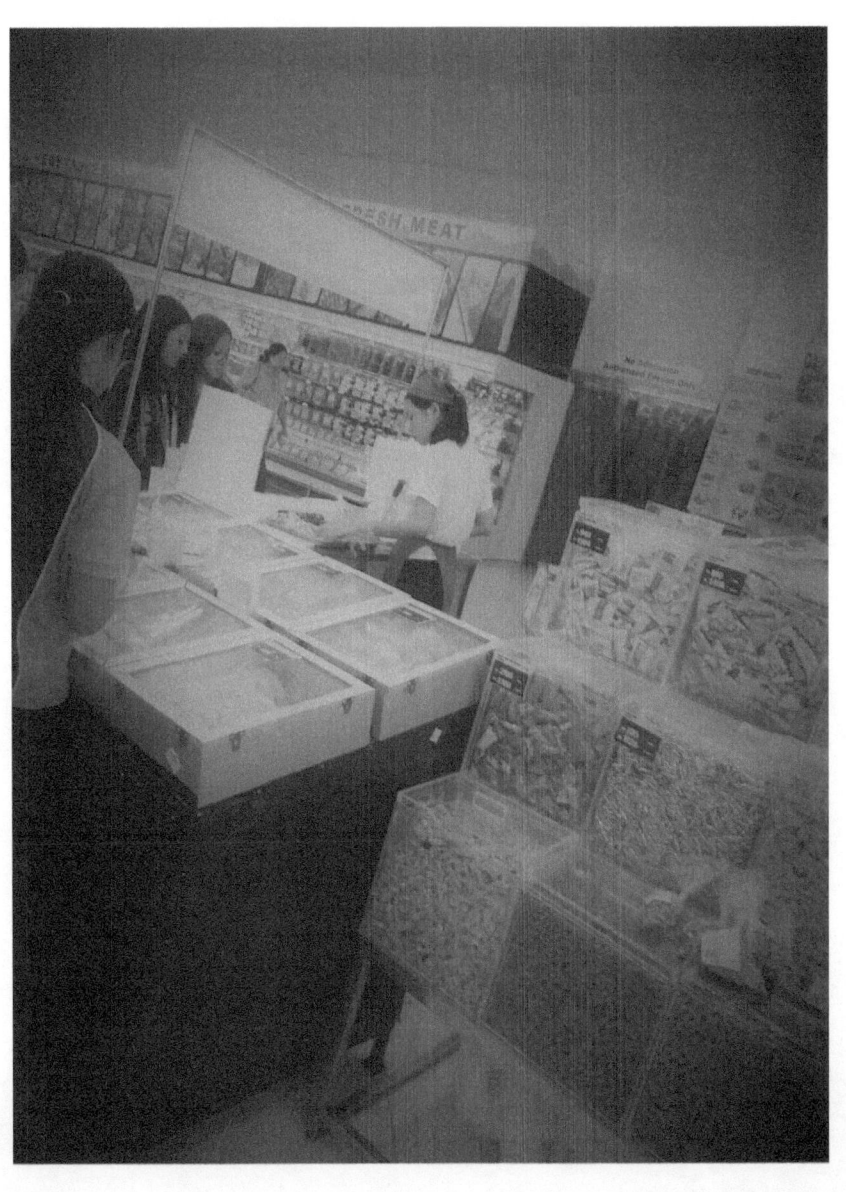

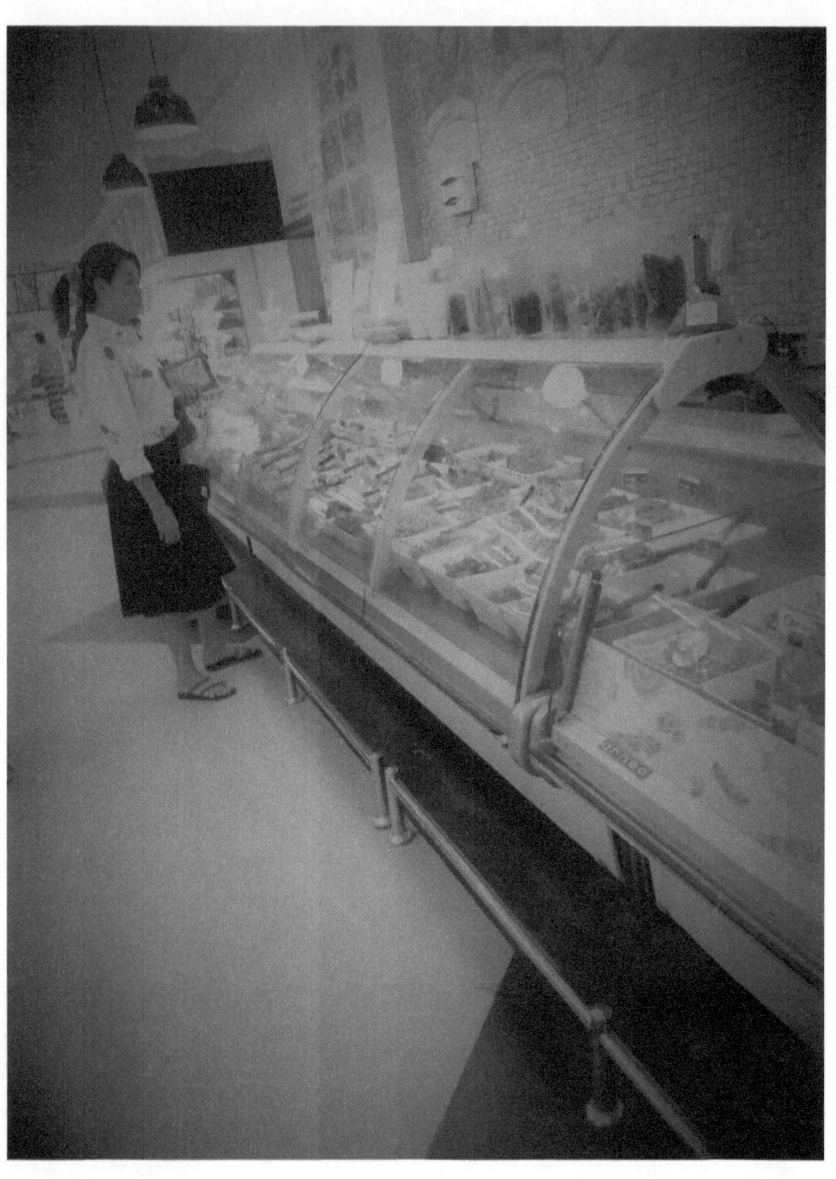

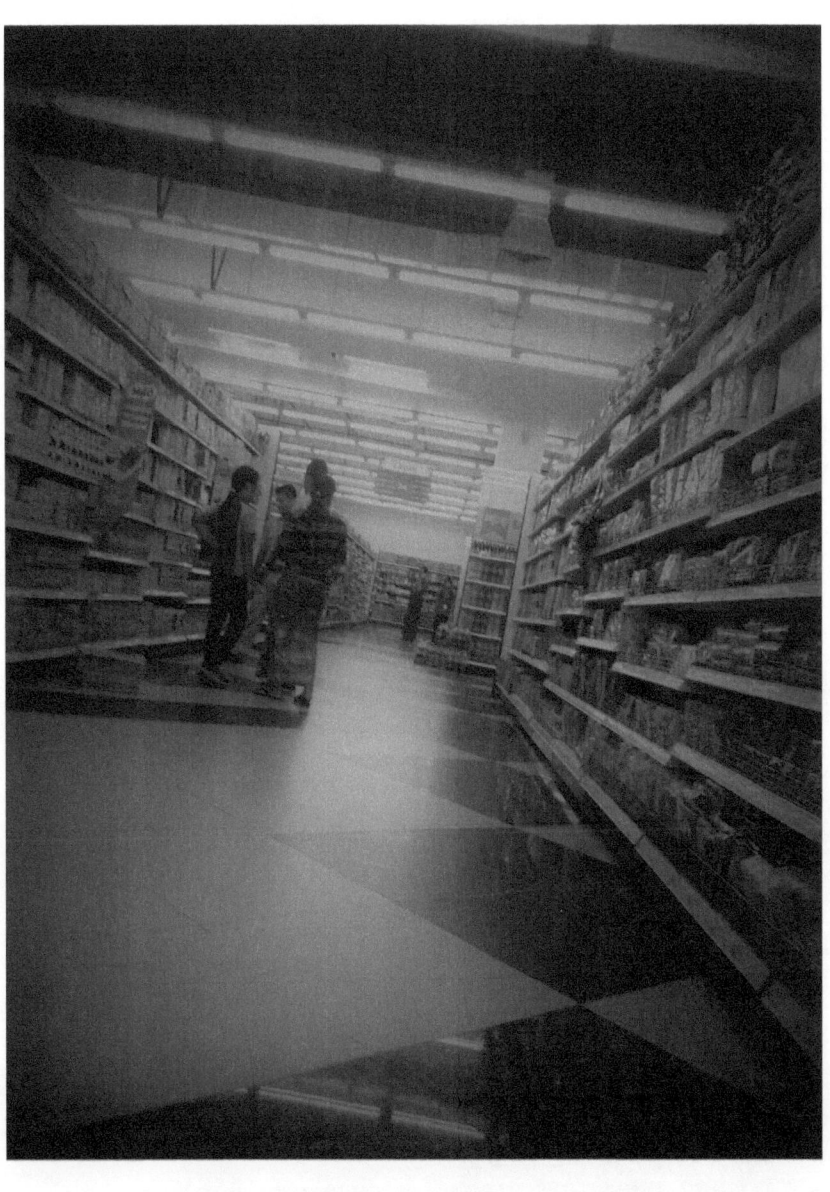

Religious Life

Religious sites are protected by polices, people that scan your body and your bad, people you do not notice. Not in a temple, like here in the first photo taken in Nay Pyi Taw, like in airport. People on which you rely with you safety and yet are like ghost. Faceless. But in the pagodas you go to pray and in the almost empty city of Nay Pyi Taw going to pray may automatically mean a quiet surrounding.

In Yangon, like in the remaining photos, the devotion is a clear, calm show of faith. It means having a break, to sleep in a holy place or just while working to keep it clean. It is helping people in wheel chairs to be able to visit the temple. While to counterpoint the quiet atmosphere inside there is always a bustling life outside.

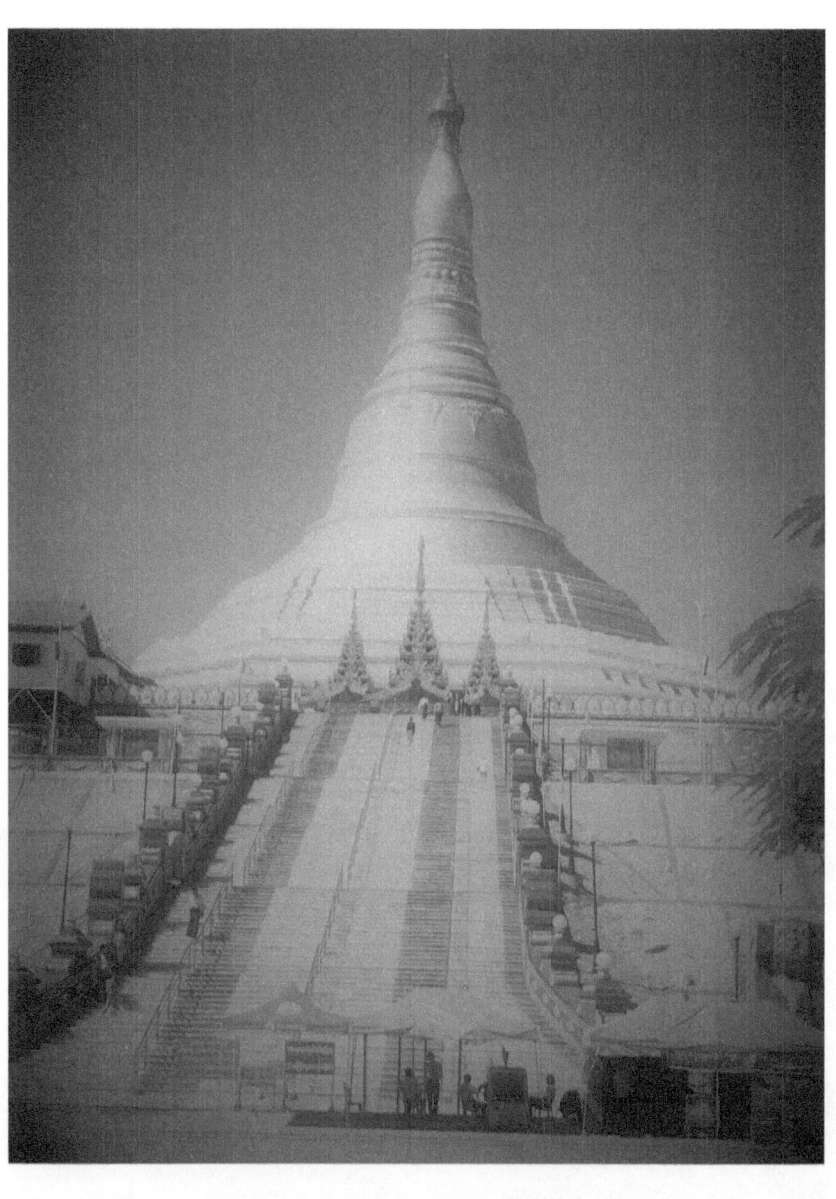

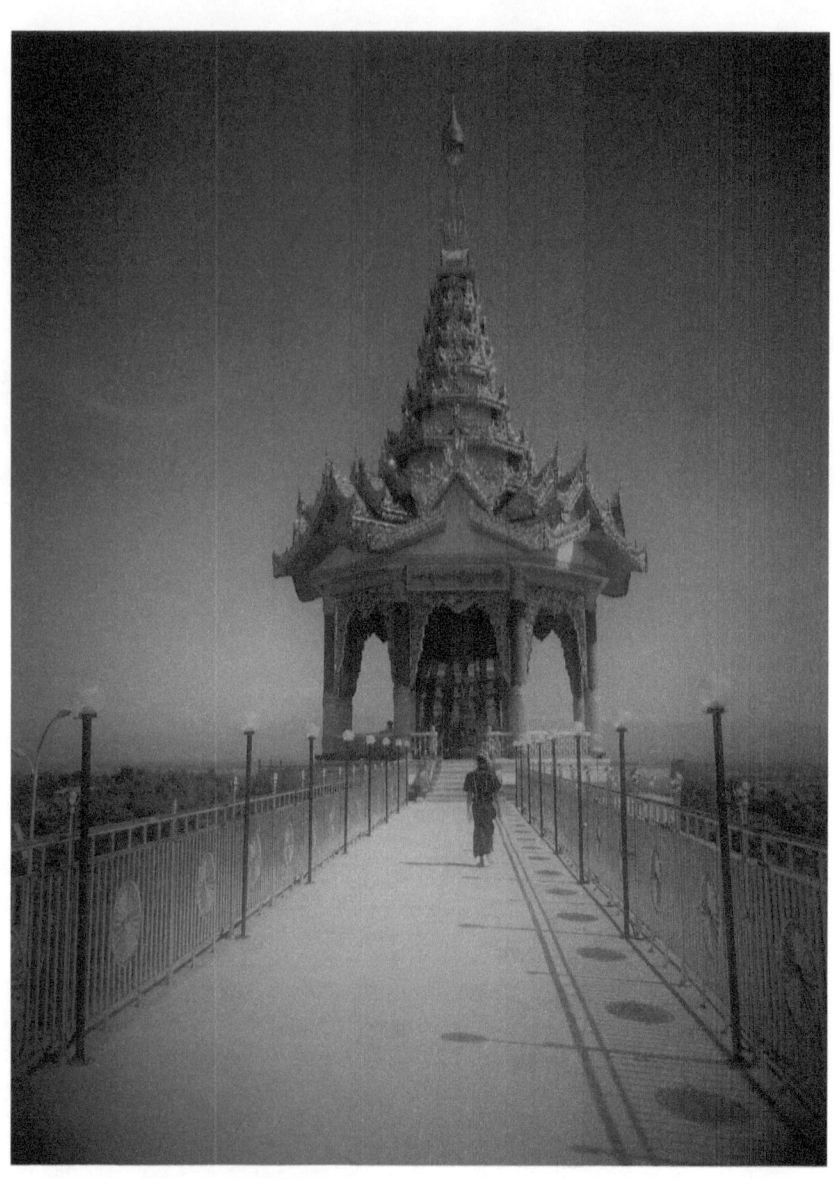

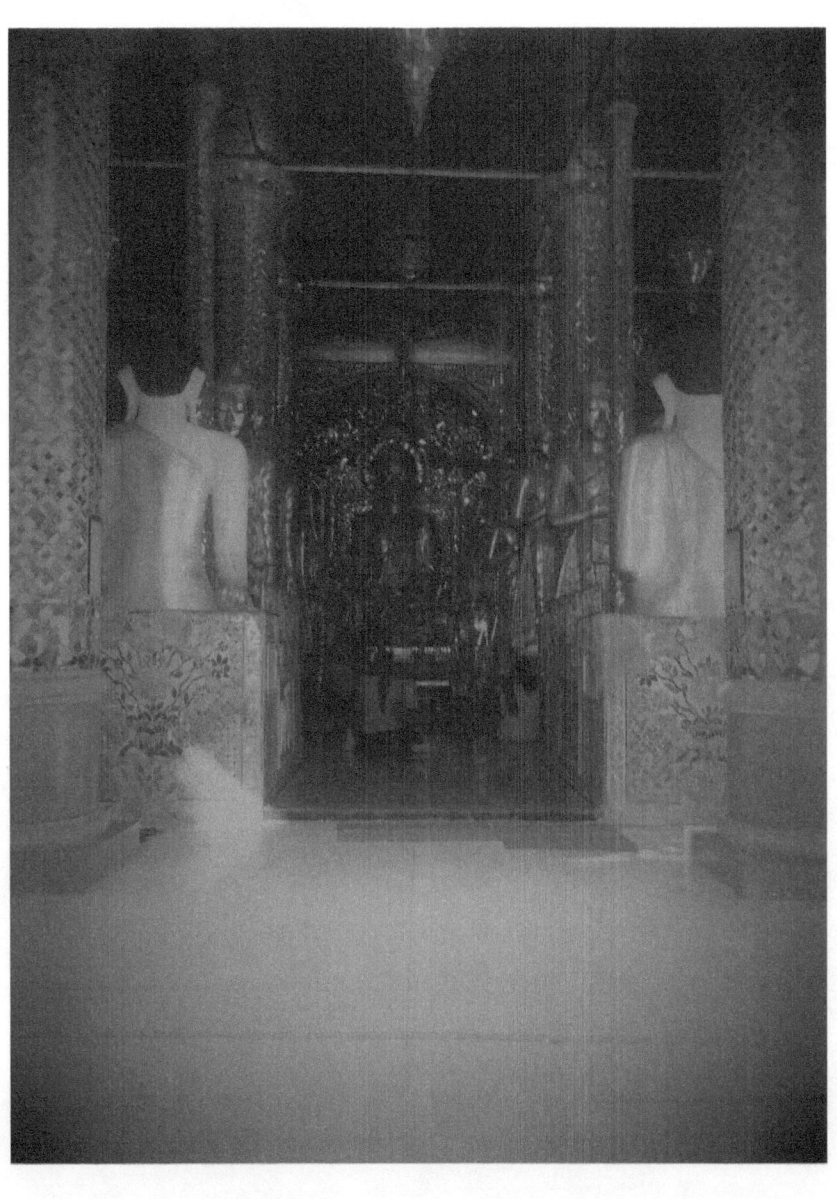

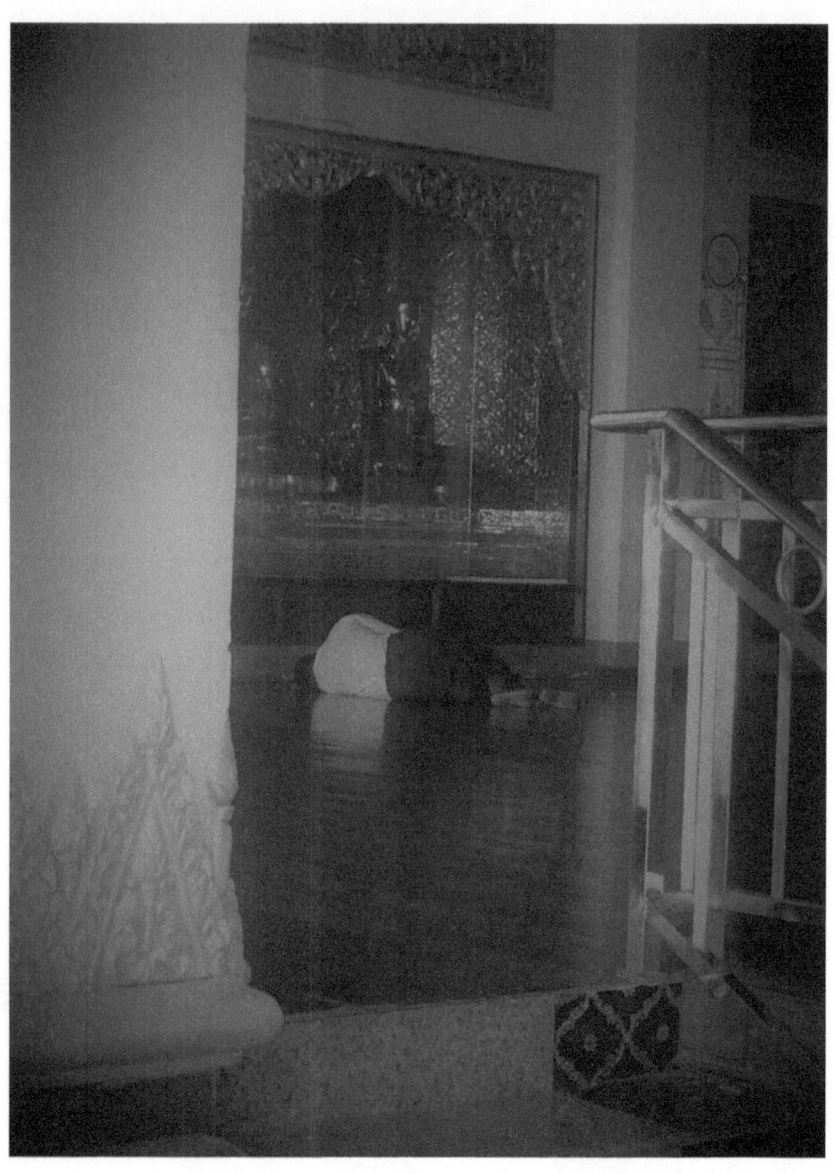

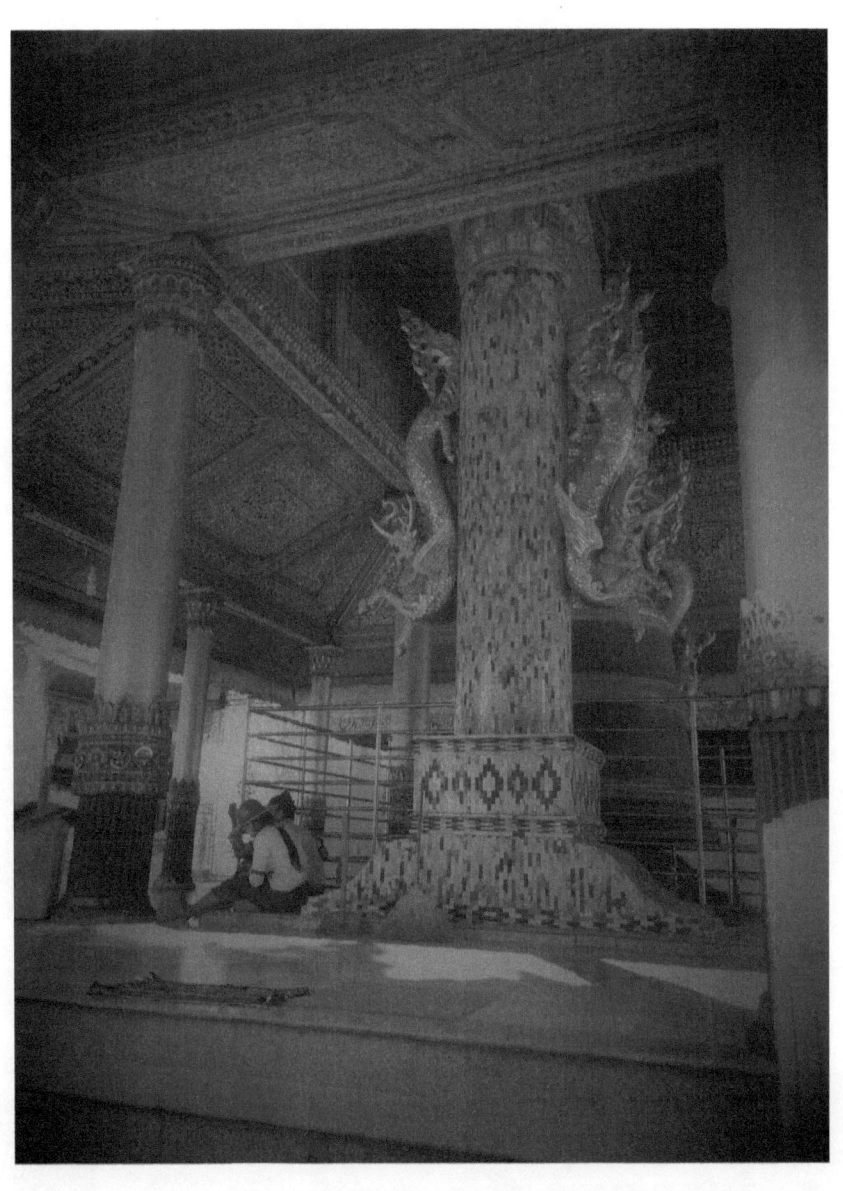

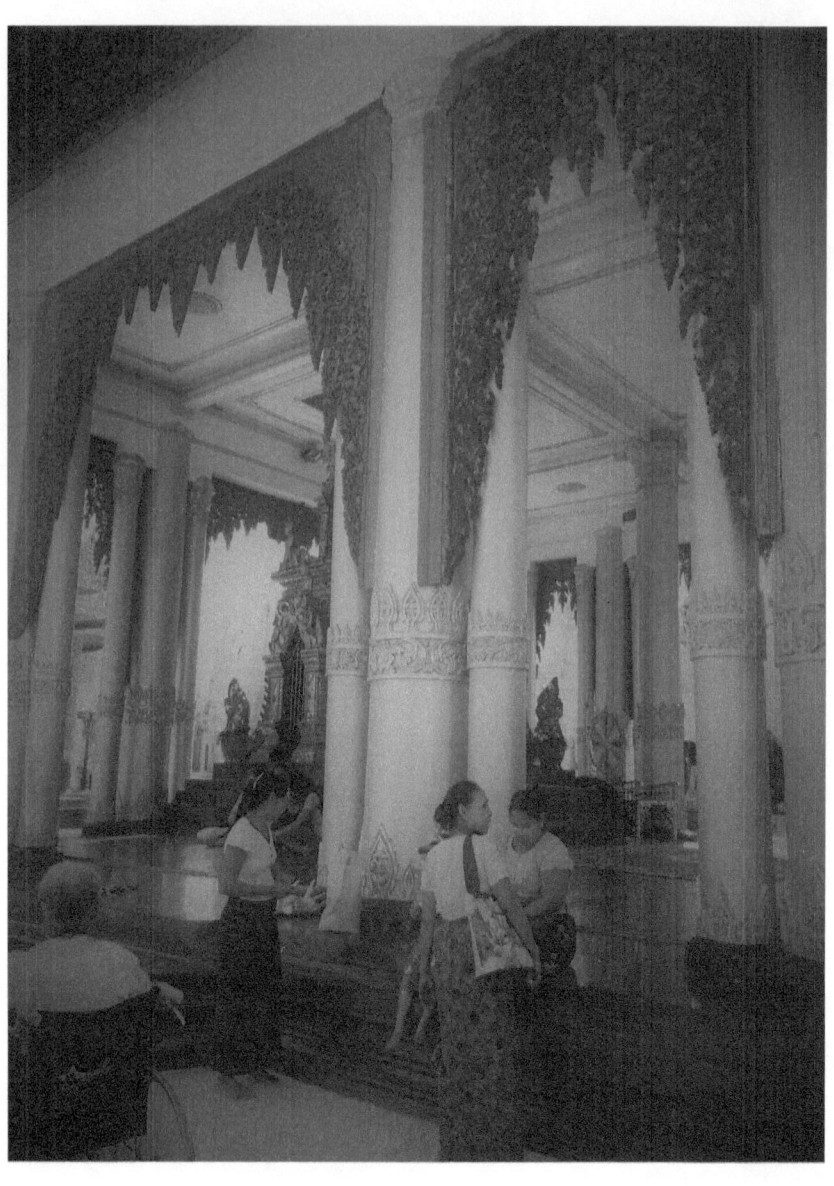

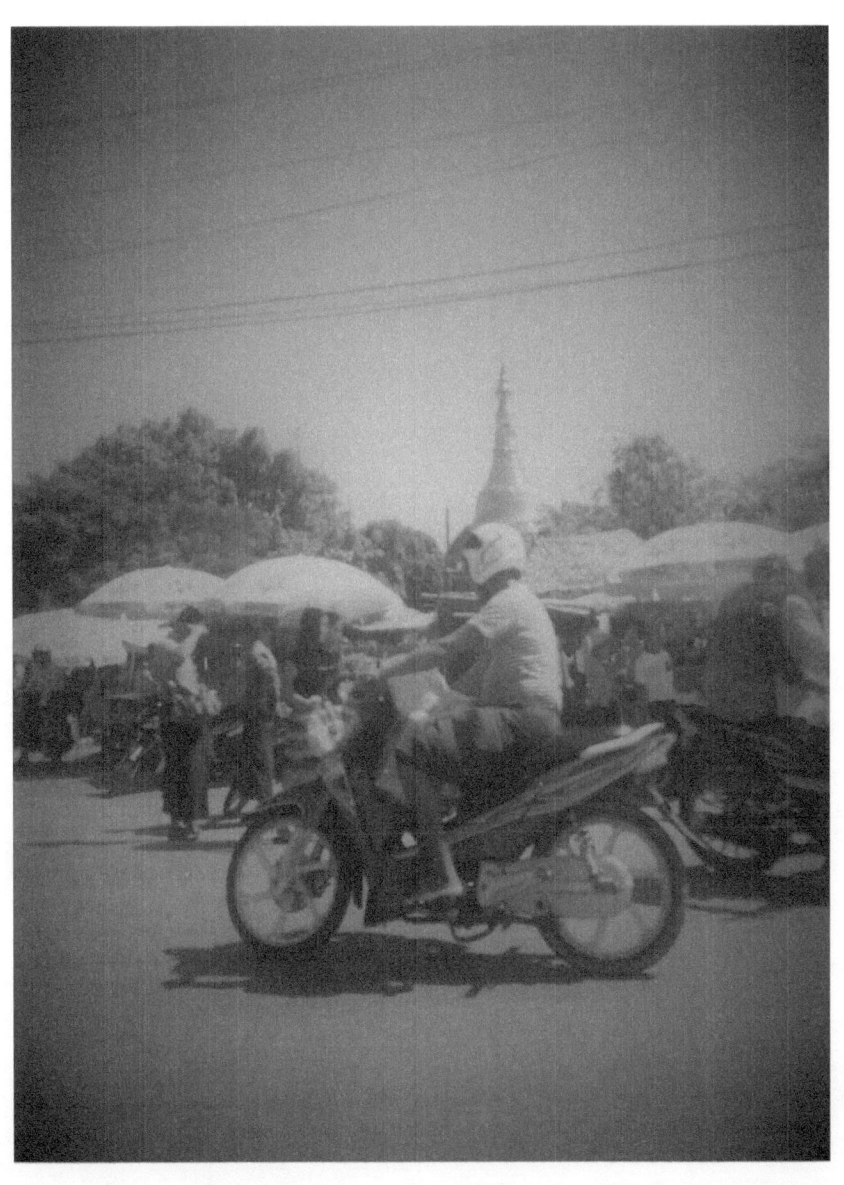

Mobility

A developing country is nothing without the crazy traffic, the millions of motorbikes and the wild strange vehicles.

Myanmar is not different.

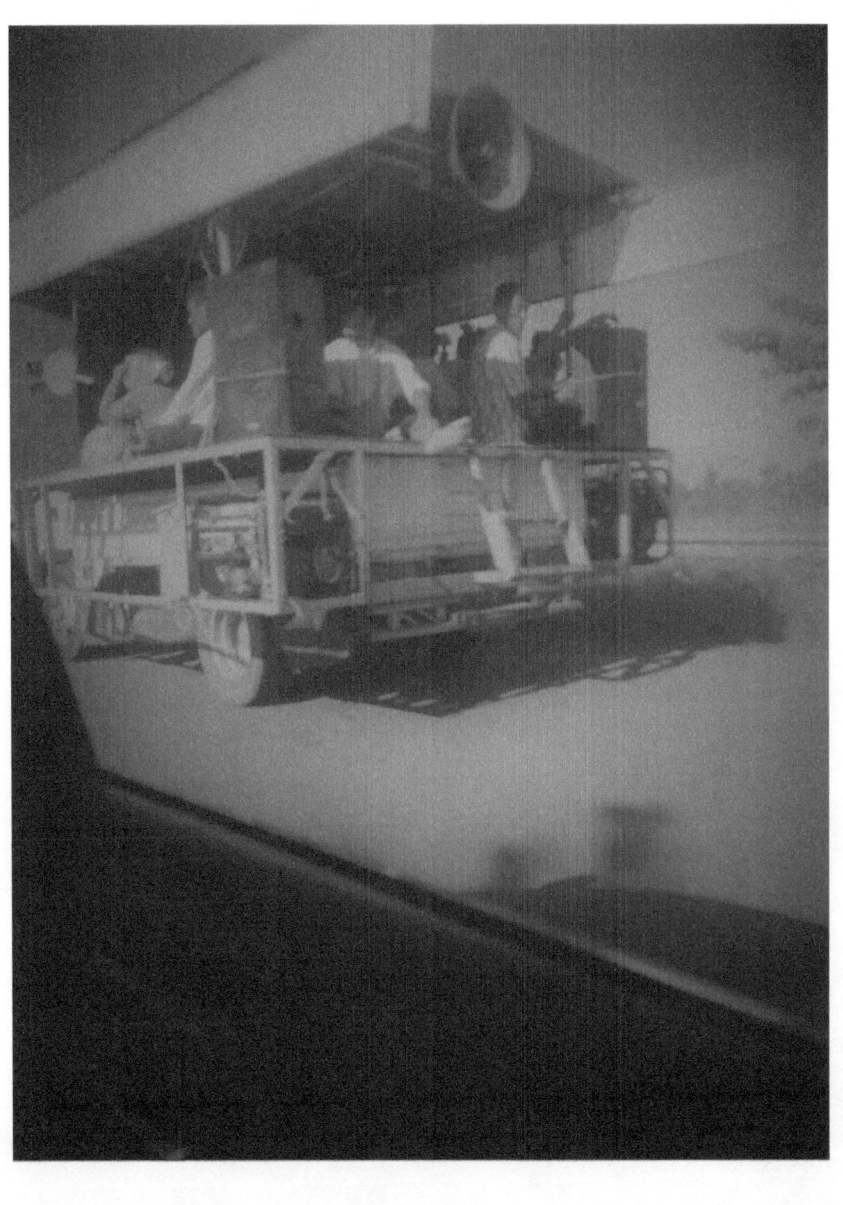

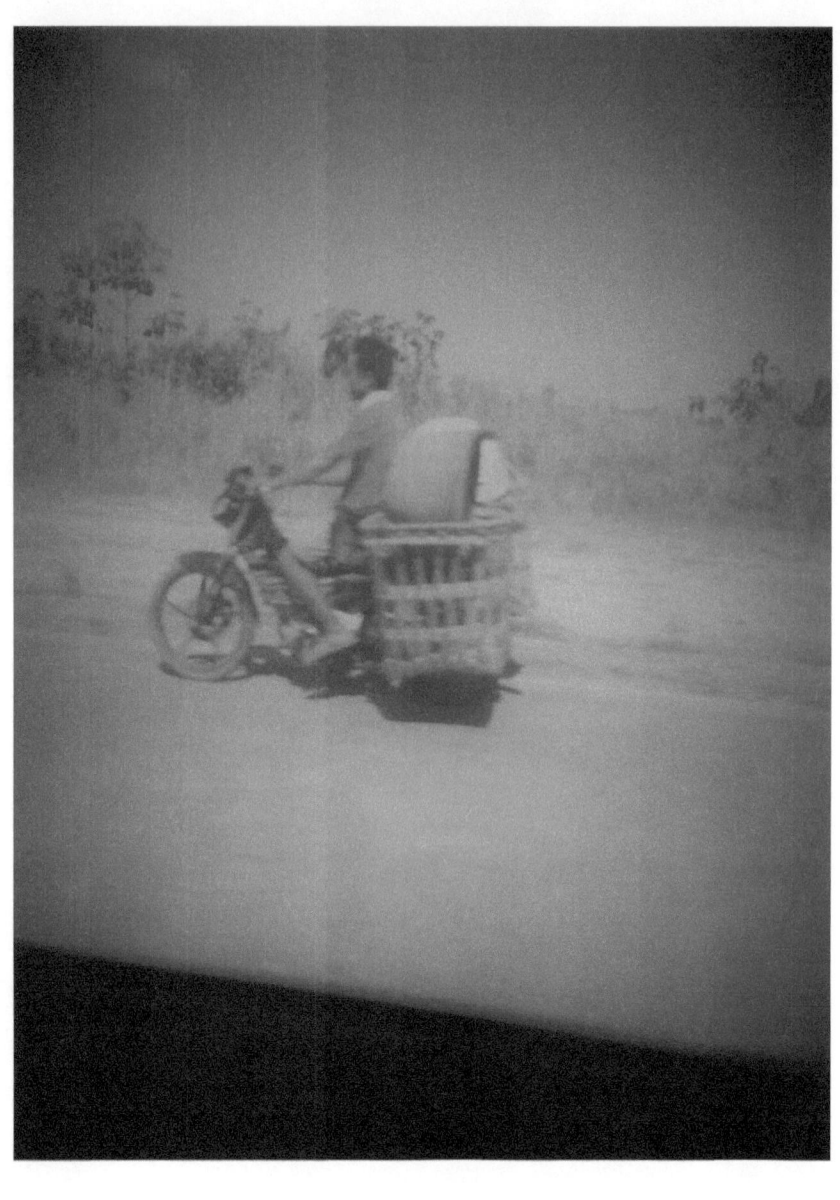

www.ingramcontent.com/pod-product-compliance
Lightning Source LLC
Chambersburg PA
CBHW031518210526
45464CB00007B/2964